GAME ON!

SUPER SMASH BROS.

JESSICA RUSICK

Checkerboard
Library

An Imprint of Abdo Publishing
abdobooks.com

abdobooks.com

Published by Abdo Publishing, a division of ABDO, PO Box 398166, Minneapolis, Minnesota 55439. Copyright © 2022 by Abdo Consulting Group, Inc. International copyrights reserved in all countries. No part of this book may be reproduced in any form without written permission from the publisher. Checkerboard Library™ is a trademark and logo of Abdo Publishing.

Printed in the United States of America, North Mankato, Minnesota
052021
092021

THIS BOOK CONTAINS
RECYCLED MATERIALS

Design: Aruna Rangarajan, Mighty Media, Inc.
Production: Mighty Media, Inc.
Editor: Rebecca Felix
Design Elements: Shutterstock Images
Cover Photograph: AntMan3001/Flickr
Interior Photographs: Alpha/Flickr, p. 16; AntMan3001/Flickr, pp. 18-19, 23, 29 (top); Courtesy of The Strong, Rochester, New York, p. 11; Farley Santos/Flickr, pp. 5, 21, 29 (bottom right); Instacodez/Flickr, p. 25 (bottom); Handout/Getty Images, p. 27; Jordan Strauss/AP Images, p. 13; Mighty Media, p. 4; Paul Boxley/Flickr, p. 6; Phillip Jeffrey/Flickr, p. 24; Picasa 2.7/Flickr, pp. 7, 28 (bottom left); Ric Francis/AP Images, p. 9; Shutterstock Images, p. 25; Sophie Lenaerts/Cédric Simon/Flickr, pp. 15, 28-29

Library of Congress Control Number: 2020949733

Publisher's Cataloging-in-Publication Data
Names: Rusick, Jessica, author.
Title: Super Smash Bros. / by Jessica Rusick
Description: Minneapolis, Minnesota : Abdo Publishing, 2022 | Series: Game On! | Includes online resources and index.
Identifiers: ISBN 9781532195822 (lib. bdg.) | ISBN 9781644945506 (pbk.) | ISBN 9781098216559 (ebook)
Subjects: LCSH: Video games--Juvenile literature. | Super Smash Bros. (Game)--Juvenile literature. | Nintendo video games--Juvenile literature. | Hand-to-hand fighting--Juvenile literature. | Video games and children--Juvenile literature.
Classification: DDC 794.8--dc23

NOTE TO READERS

Video games that depict shooting or other violent acts should be subject to adult discretion and awareness that exposure to such acts may affect players' perceptions of violence in the real world.

CONTENTS

SMASH BROS. SHOWDOWN

Four popular video game characters stand on a rocky **stage** that floats above waterfalls. A countdown ends and the characters attack one another at lightning speed. They hurl items at each other and try to blast one another off the stage. Who will win this *Super Smash Bros.* battle, and who will be eliminated by **knockout**?

Super Smash Bros. is the best-selling fighting video game **franchise** of all time. In each title, players battle as their favorite characters from video game company Nintendo and other video game franchises. These franchises include *Mario*, *Pokémon*, *Animal Crossing*, and *PAC-MAN*.

> ### LOGO LINES
> The *Super Smash Bros.* logo is a circle with two crossed lines. These lines represent the **crossover** fights between characters in the *Super Smash Bros.* series.

Super Smash Bros. has been a fan favorite for more than 20 years. And, it's still going strong. Each new game features more characters and special features than the last!

SMASH BROS. MASTERMIND

Super Smash Bros. creator Masahiro Sakurai was born in Tokyo, Japan, in 1970. At age 19, Sakurai began working for HAL Laboratory. This company helped develop games for Nintendo. In 1996, while working at HAL, Sakurai had an idea for a new type of fighting game.

At the time, fighting games featured only two-player fights. To win, a player **depleted** the other player's health bar. Sakurai wanted to make a game with four-players fights. And, there would be no health bars. Instead, a player would win by launching opponents off the **stage**.

Sakurai believed his fighting game would be perfect the Nintendo 64 (N64) **console**. The N64 was the first home gaming

KIRBY

In 1989, Sakurai designed the character Kirby (*pictured*). Kirby went on to star in several Nintendo games. He is also a character in every *Super Smash Bros.* game.

Masahiro Sakurai worked a part-time job in high school to earn money to buy video games.

console with a stick controller. This allowed players to move characters with greater accuracy. Sakurai wanted his game to take advantage of this feature.

BUILDING THE GAME

Sakurai asked HAL president Satoru Iwata to help him develop his fighting game. Sakurai worked on game planning and design. Iwata worked on **programming**.

The men created a **prototype** game called *Dragon King: The Fighting Game* in 1996. Its fighters were faceless. But Sakurai thought players would enjoy the game more if it used established Nintendo characters as fighters!

Sakurai asked Nintendo for permission to use its characters in the game. Nintendo said no. But Sakurai and Iwata used Nintendo characters anyway to redevelop the prototype. In 1998, the men showed it to Nintendo.

Nintendo executives loved the prototype! The company gave HAL permission to develop a game using Nintendo characters. *Super Smash Bros.* was born.

PLAYING TO LEARN

Sakurai often plays new video games. He believes he can learn something new about game design from each one.

Before *Dragon King: The Fighting Game* got its name, its developers called the game "4-player Battle Royal."

SUPER SMASH BROS.

Super Smash Bros. was released for the N64 in 1999. The game's main **mode** was Versus. In Versus mode, up to four players could fight each other at once. They battled on **stages** inspired by Nintendo games.

Versus mode featured eight base Nintendo characters. These included Mario, Link, Kirby, and Pikachu. Players could unlock four more characters by playing the game's single-player mode. In this mode, one player fought against opponents controlled by the game's **central processing unit (CPU)**. These characters are called CPU opponents.

The N64 controller allowed players to move characters more easily than in other fighting games. Fun, easy gameplay made *Super Smash Bros.* an instant hit! It became one of the N64's best-selling games.

Nintendo sold more than 5 million copies of *Super Smash Bros.* in the game's first year.

A SMASH HIT

After the success of *Super Smash Bros.*, Nintendo wanted to release a **sequel**. Once again, Sakurai led the game's development. He added 14 characters to the new game, called *Super Smash Bros. Melee*. These included Bowser from *Mario* and Mewtwo from *Pokémon*. The game also featured new **stages**, new items, and three single-player **modes**.

Melee **debuted** in 2001 on the Nintendo GameCube **console**. It sold 1 million copies within two months of its release. It would later become the best-selling GameCube game of all time!

Melee players began gathering to play the game at unofficial tournaments. These tournaments grew in popularity. From 2003 to 2006, *Melee* was part of **Major League Gaming's** circuit. Players worldwide competed to win money in *Melee* tournaments!

Sakurai (*right*) attended the *Super Smash Bros.* Invitational in 2018.

BIG-TIME BRAWL

Although *Melee* was a hit, the GameCube had sold poorly. But *Melee*'s success helped keep *Super Smash Bros.*' popularity alive. In 2006, Nintendo released the Wii **console**. Fans hoped a new *Super Smash Bros.* game would be created to go with it. Nintendo had plans to do just that!

Sakurai's former HAL boss Iwata had become president of Nintendo in 2002. And in 2003, Sakurai had left HAL to start his own video game company, Sora Ltd. In 2005, Iwata invited Sakurai to direct and design a new *Super Smash Bros.* game. It was called *Super Smash Bros. Brawl*.

Brawl **debuted** in 2008. In the United States, the game sold faster than any other Nintendo game in history. Worldwide, it became one of the Wii's best-selling games.

NINTENDO WII

The Wii featured a different controller than previous Nintendo consoles. Many Wii games also featured motion capture gameplay.

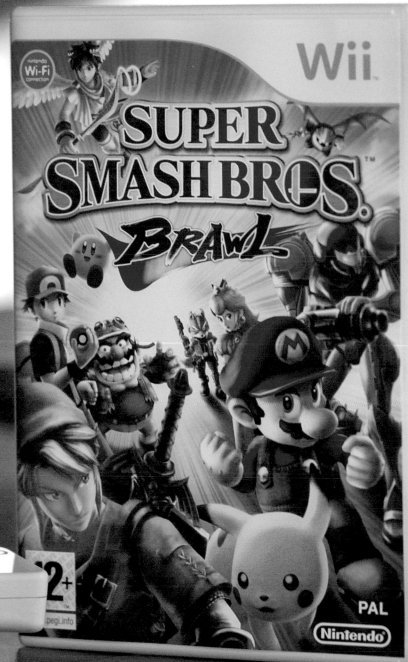

Four different controllers can be used at once to play *Brawl*. These are the Wii Remote (*pictured*), Wii Remote with Nunchuk, GameCube controller, and Classic Controller.

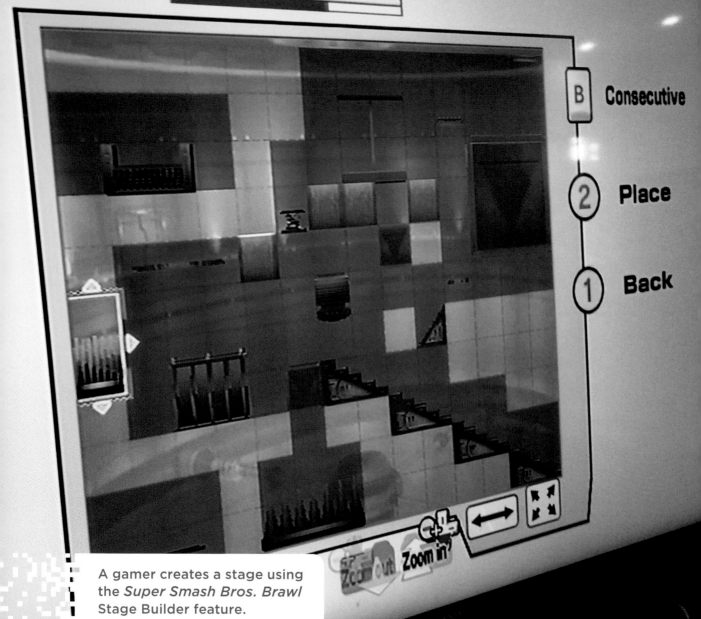

A gamer creates a stage using the *Super Smash Bros. Brawl* Stage Builder feature.

Brawl had 37 playable characters, including 16 new ones. And for the first time the **franchise's** history, some characters were from non-Nintendo games! These were Solid Snake from *Metal Gear* and Sonic from *Sonic the Hedgehog*.

Another first in *Brawl* was allowing players to take screenshots of gameplay. They could share these with other players. They could also record matches.

Stage Builder was another new feature. This allowed players to design their own stages. Players first chose between several backgrounds. Then, they placed items such as platforms, spikes, ladders, and tunnels on their stages.

Brawl also introduced Final Smash to make brawls more **unpredictable**. This feature caused an item called a Smash Ball to float across the stage at **random** times. Players raced to break the ball. Whoever broke it got to unleash a powerful move called the Final Smash!

CREATING CROSSOVERS

Fans love *Super Smash Bros.* games' **crossovers** with other video game **franchises**. To use a third-party character, Nintendo must get permission from the company that developed the character. Sakurai and his team then tweak the character's appearance and movements to blend into *Super Smash Bros.* The company that owns the character approves these tweaks.

Other video games are also incorporated as *Super Smash Bros.* Trophies. These are digital statues players collect by completing certain tasks. Trophies are characters, items, or other details from a video game franchise. Sakurai often decides which **stages**, items, and Trophies to include in a *Smash Bros.* game.

ASSIST TROPHIES

Brawl introduced Assist Trophies to the *Super Smash Bros.* universe. When picked up, these reveal a **random** character that helps the user fight. The Assist Trophy characters are different from the game's playable characters.

Super Smash Bros. characters are called "fighters." Some fighters share similar abilities with other fighters. These characters are called "echo fighters."

A FOURTH INSTALLMENT

In 2014, Nintendo **debuted** *Super Smash Bros.* for Wii U. The game introduced the **franchise's** first eight-player brawls. It also allowed players to create and play as **avatars** called Miis.

Downloadable content (DLC) was another franchise first. It allowed players to buy new players and **stages** on their devices.

ICONIC ADDITION

Iconic video game character PAC-MAN was added to the lineup in *Super Smash Bros. for Wii U.* A stage inspired by the game *PAC-MAN* also debuted. This stage scrolls through a colorful landscape.

Amiibos were also a new addition. These were physical figurines of characters in the game. Players who bought Amiibos could wirelessly connect them to their games. In the game, players could then **customize** their Amiibo characters' moves and teach them how to fight!

When Amiibos first debuted, they would often sell out on pre-order before even reaching stores!

THE ULTIMATE GAME

In 2015, Nintendo tasked Sakurai with developing a *Super Smash Bros.* game for its newest **console**, the Switch. The Switch was Nintendo's first **hybrid** console. It could transform from a home console to a handheld console!

Sakurai decided the game, *Super Smash Bros. Ultimate*, would include every character that had ever appeared in a *Super Smash Bros.* game, plus new ones. Each old character's graphics, movements, and outfits were **updated** to look just right in the new game.

Ultimate was released in 2018. Many fans and critics said it was **franchise's** best game yet. In November 2019, it became the best-selling fighting game of all time!

WORLD OF LIGHT

Ultimate included a new **mode** called World of Light. In this mode, a villain named Galeem has turned most of the *Super Smash Bros.* fighters into his puppets. The fighters' spirits are trapped in these puppets. Players must fight the puppets to free the spirits and defeat Galeem.

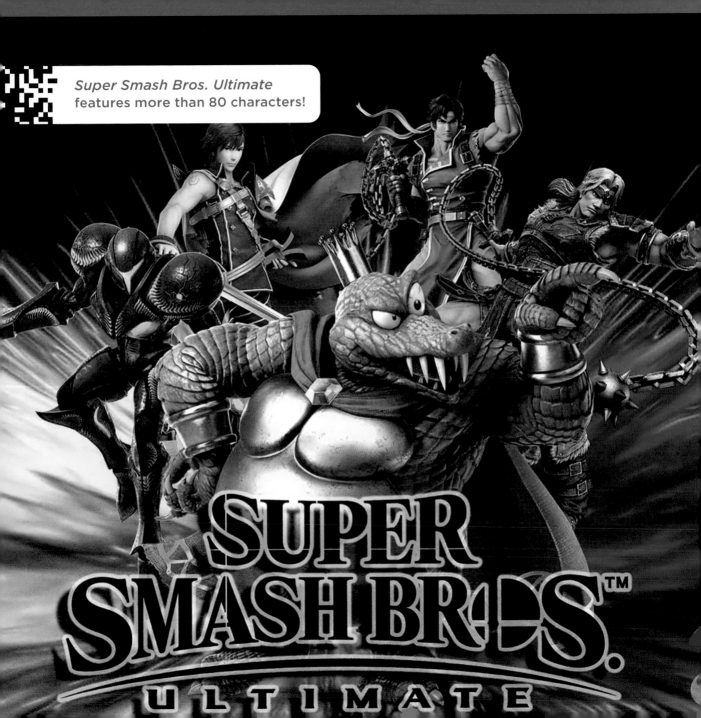

Super Smash Bros. Ultimate features more than 80 characters!

SUPER SMASH BROS.™
ULTIMATE

LEVEL UP!

Super Smash Bros.: Basic to Ultimate

Super Smash Bros. Ultimate was a hit with fans. In its first week, it sold more than 5 million copies worldwide! By 2020, it was the third most popular title on the Nintendo Switch.

1999

SUPER SMASH BROS.

+ **Console**: Nintendo 64

+ Players: 1 to 4

+ 12 playable characters

+ 9 **stages**

+ 21 items, including Fire Flower (shoots fire at other players) and Star (makes a player invincible for a limited time)

2018

SUPER SMASH BROS. ULTIMATE

+ **Console**: Nintendo Switch

+ Players: 1 to 8

+ 74 playable characters in base game, plus more with DLC

+ 103 **stages** in base game, plus more with DLC

+ 87 items, including Beetle (grabs onto another player and pulls them upward) and Super Leaf (allows a player to **hover**)

NINTENDO SWITCH

The Nintendo Switch has a Joy-Con controller on each side. These can be removed for different **modes** of play.

Characters Luigi, Sonic, Kirby, and more battle on a rocky stage in *Ultimate.*

A SMASHING SUCCESS

Super Smash Bros. Ultimate has continued to add new content with DLC **updates**. An update in October 2020 introduced *Minecraft* characters to the game. Players could also play on a new *Minecraft*-inspired **stage**.

Fans looked forward what updates would come next. And, they wondered what was in store for the **franchise's** future. In 2020, some gaming experts **predicted** another new *Super Smash Bros.* game would be released in a few years' time. But that same year, Sakurai said he had no plans to work on a new video game. This made fans wonder if the game's creator would soon retire.

Throughout its history, *Super Smash Bros.* has been a hit with players and critics alike. Gamers everywhere love the franchise's ever-expanding list of characters and features. The games' easy-to-learn gameplay and sense of fun hook new players and keep old ones coming back for more.

Excited fans cheer on their favorite characters during a *Super Smash Bros.* Invitational tournament.

KIRBY

ZELDA

FOX MCCLOUD

TIMELINE

1998

Sakurai and Satoru Iwata show a prototype fighting game featuring Nintendo characters to Nintendo. HAL begins developing *Super Smash Bros.* for the N64.

1989

Sakurai begins working at HAL Laboratory.

1970

Super Smash Bros. creator Masahiro Sakurai is born in Tokyo, Japan.

1996

Sakurai has an idea for a new type of fighting game that will feature four-player battles.

2001

Super Smash Bros. Melee is released for the GameCube.

2018

Super Smash Bros. Ultimate is released for the Switch. It features every character that appeared in *Super Smash Bros.*

1999

Super Smash Bros. is released for the N64.

2014

Super Smash Bros. debuts for the Wii U.

2020

An update introduces *Minecraft* characters to the game.

2008

Super Smash Bros. Brawl is released for the Wii.

GLOSSARY

avatar—an icon or figure representing a player in video games.

central processing unit (CPU)—the part of a computer that executes instructions of a computer program.

console—an electronic system used to play video games.

crossover—when otherwise separated fictional characters or media in two or more video games meet and interact with each other.

customize—to make something to order and that is one of a kind.

debut (DAY-byoo)—to first appear.

deplete—to use up something or someone's supplies or energy.

downloadable—able to be transferred from a computer network to a single computer or device.

franchise—a series of related works, such as movies or video games, that feature the same characters.

hybrid—combining two or more functions or ways of operation.

knockout—a term used in fighting video games to describe one character hitting another character in a powerful enough way to end the fight.

Major League Gaming—an organization hosting professional competitions of multiplayer video games.

mode—a way of operating or using a system.

predict—to guess something ahead of time on the basis of observation, experience, or reasoning. If something cannot be guessed in this way, it is called unpredictable.

program—to write computer software.

prototype—an early model of a product on which future versions can be modeled.

random—lacking a definite plan or pattern.

sequel—a movie, game, or other work that continues the story of a previous work.

stage—the on-screen space available to players during a video game.

update—to make something more modern or up-to-date. An update is a more modern or up-to-date form of something.

ONLINE RESOURCES

Booklinks
NONFICTION NETWORK
FREE! ONLINE NONFICTION RESOURCES

To learn more about *Super Smash Bros.*, please visit **abdobooklinks.com** or scan this QR code. These links are routinely monitored and updated to provide the most current information available.

INDEX